THE SMART WOMAN

GUIDE TO

NETWORKING

DARINE BENAMARA

THE SMART WOMAN GUIDE TO

NETWORKING

A POWERFUL GUIDE TO BUILD, USE & MAINTAIN YOUR NETWORK

1st edition.

Published by EasyPublishing
Toronto, Canada

Design by Darine BenAmara

ISBN-13: 978-1726202442
ISBN-10: 1726202445

IN MEMORY OF MY CHERISHED AUNT
AND BELOVED GRANDMA

TO MY MOM
for raising me to believe that anything was possible

TO MY HUSBAND
for making everything possible

TO ALL THE WOMEN
empowered and empowering

CONTENTS

A LETTER TO YOU

Hello Smart Woman,

You're reading this because you are a tenacious woman with big ambitions.

You know networking plays an important part in your success. You've attended networking events, taken the bold step to introduce yourself to new people and share your story and professional aspirations. You've distributed your business cards and brought home a bunch; sent follow-up emails and maybe even taken the extra step and made some calls. Yet, despite the time and energy invested, you don't experience enough return. If you enjoyed it at first, you don't anymore. If you had confidence at first, you've somehow landed up feeling less confident, more directionless and less eager to keepin' on.

Believe it or not, there is a way to course-correct. Networking can be incredibly rewarding and an experience that brings you joy and inspiration.

I discovered networking when I moved to Canada in 2012. I was a recent graduate full of ambitions. Many people advised me to invest time in networking if I was serious about building a career in Canada. So, I did what you would naturally assume. I attended several events, spoke to people, collected business cards from anyone I had an interaction with. I networked morning, noon and night, on weekdays and weekends. But, like some of you, my career wasn't going anywhere and I grew increasingly frustrated. I didn't know what wasn't working. I started to find fault within myself for why my connections failed to generate value. I began to

2

blame my demeanour, fault my looks, and discredit my experience. It impacted my self-esteem and made me feel less confident in my ability to lead, persuade and influence those around me.

One day, I decided to cut the self-imposed judgment and criticism and reflect on a question that was asked to me some time ago: "Do you network smart or do you network hard?" I realized that I had approached networking the way I had always done everything – by working very hard and thinking that brute effort would generate positive results.

What I learned was if I wanted different results, I needed to change my approach to networking. So, I started asking questions, I did my research and figured out that if I wanted to network effectively, I had to change my mindset. Networking is not about being social but about being strategic. Networking is not about meeting as many people as possible in the room but rather to make a few valuable connections. And foremost, it is about building mutually beneficial relationships.

The changes I made landed me one of my most coveted roles to date: an opportunity to work for one of the advisors to President Barack Obama.

Where did I take my strength from? Other women. For the past 7 years, I have been working with women around the world from whom I have learned so much. Many of them are badass women with years of experience and a certain notoriety. Surprisingly, regardless what part of the world they live in and no matter how high in the hierarchy they are, the postulation is the same: women struggle at networking. It seems much easier for men to network, which is no surprise when you realize that the great majority of executive positions and high-level businesses are still dominated by men. So as women, how can we approach them and do a better job of talking our way to success?

In one word, the answer is "strategy". We women need to be more strategic and intentional networkers to make up for our upbringing. Few of us are born networkers, but anyone – introvert, extrovert, or in-between – can learn to master this critical skill.

The Smart Woman Guide to Networking is the outcome of several conversations with thousands of women around the world, listening to their struggles and sharing my own, realizing that networking can be awkward, uncomfortable and time-consuming for most of us.

I designed this guide to give women the tools to thrive and growth; and help you become a networking hustler. Yes, it is possible. You can do it now! No more time to waste, it's time for action.

INTRODUCTION

If you don't like
something, change it.
If you can't change it,
change your attitude.

- MAYA ANGELOU

No matter what profession we are in, no matter what country or what culture we come from, networking is the fuel that accelerates success, and it is an especially important skill for women.

Many of us are intimidated by the word "networking" because we feel like we don't have the personality type and/or skills to stand out in a room full of strangers. The word networking can leave a bad taste in our mouth, as we are not sure where to start, what to say, or how to maintain relationships.

We often make the mistake of pouring our energy into networking only at a time when we are seeking new opportunities. By waiting to network merely when we need to, we miss out on amazing chances for professional growth. If you are looking for worthwhile connections - and Yes you ARE! - the activity must be continuous, and the sooner you start the better it is. Structured networking can make the difference between success and failure. A systematic networking effort is also personally empowering; it's one of the things we can do that directly affects success. Networking gives you control and allows you to take ownership of the development of your career and business.

Now more than ever, we need to harness this skill to gain the business advantage in order to thrive in our economy's competitive market.

I truly believe there is an art to networking and building relationships. So, this guide's sole purpose is to equip women with skills and knowledge that will boost their confidence and further their self-development. It will add great value no matter whether you are in search of employment, a professional woman who wants to make her way up the corporate ladder, a woman entrepreneur, or a woman in a leadership position.

If you follow these guidelines, you will develop your networking expertise and enhance your ability to build relationships and work with your contacts.

While strategic networking is difficult for most people, an article I read from Herminia Ibarra "Why Strategic Networking Is Harder For Women" revealed three key differences between how men and women approach networking:

1. Women have a tendency to be more easily drawn to people who are similar to us. Cultivating relationships with decision makers and influential stakeholders may feel less spontaneous and more like hard work, especially in male-dominated industries. A direct but little-understood consequence of our innate preference for hanging out with people like us is that women's work and social networks tend to overlap less frequently than men's.

2. Women tend to have smaller networks of deeper relationships, choosing to only have people in their network who share their value system, compared to men who see their network as a way to get ahead and are therefore less concerned with shared values and more interested in what the relationship can yield. As it happens, men often have some of the same people on both lists – they will play football or go for dinner with some of their work contacts. Women, by contrast, are more likely to have two separate lists: one for work activities and one for social activities. According to research conducted by LeanIn.Org and McKinsey & Co. ,

women have fewer ties than men to colleagues and cohorts both at and outside of work who can help them with their careers. Thus, maintaining separate spheres can put women at a disadvantage.

3. Making connections can also be challenging for women who want to both maximize their time at work and also dedicate time to their home life. In addition, women often feel like networking means using people as a means to an end, or they fear looking like they are bragging when they seek favor and guidance from a superior, even though it is more likely that any executive above them will be a man.

As women, we haven't been raised to be leaders, to strive in business, or ask for what we want to grow in our careers. There is not enough women in leadership roles to emulate or model, as every industry, even the ones that cater to women, are dominated by men. So when the time comes for women to exercise their leadership, demand change, or participate in a difficult conversation amongst male colleagues, as women, we tend to hold ourselves back many times because we lack the confidence and training to be successful.

Our upbringing is reflected in the data and the markets. Globally, the number of women in management positions stands between 24% and 28.5%[1] .

Inequality starts at the very first promotion. Women are significantly underrepresented throughout the corporate pipeline. From the outset, fewer women than men are hired at the entry level, despite women being 57% of recent college graduates. At every subsequent step, the representation of

---

[1] The percentage differentiates according to studies.

women continues to decline until it drops off dramatically at the senior executive level. The representation of women in senior management positions is slowly on the rise. In 2015-2016, women made up 16.3% of CEO positions and held 34.1% of senior management roles[2]. For lady bosses, the challenge remains the same. According to Inc., 48% of female entrepreneurs in the US report that a lack of available advisers and mentors limits their professional growth.

Self-awareness is key.

A lack of confidence and self-awareness is deep-rooted and has serious professional implications. A Women's Leadership Study by KPMG revealed over 67% of women expressing need for greater support building confidence to feel like they can be leaders. Lack of confidence amongst women can manifest in career hindering ways. Nine in 10 women refrain from asking for sponsors because they aren't confident in making the ask. The same study proved a lack of confidence has prevented 79% of women from seeking mentors, asking for access to senior leadership (76%), pursuing a job opportunity beyond their experience (73%), asking for a career path plan (69%), requesting a promotion (65%), a raise (61%), or a new role or position (56%).

Networking is an agency women can adopt to create the community and opportunities required for career and business success.

---

[2] Workplace Gender Equality Agency, Australia's Gender Equality Scorecard: Key Findings from the Workplace Gender Equality Agency's 2015-16 Reporting Data (2016).

How can networking help?

Networking is about identifying opportunities. More than 80% of employment opportunities are filled by recommendations. People are more likely to invest their time to probe a potential candidate for an opportunity if they have been referred by someone favored or are connected to people who are well respected and creditable. So, success in business is definitely about whom you know.

Most of us realize that networking is essential for getting things done in our day-to-day jobs and for our longer-term career growth. Who we know and connect with directly influences our exposure to individuals, information or opportunities.

Your network is made up of personal and professional relationships that help you envision the future, craft and pitch your ideas, and obtain the resources necessary to move forward your career or to grow your business. Whether you are in a job, looking for a job, or in business for yourself, networking can help you tap into your fullest potential.

Networking does not need to feel transactional, nor should it be approached in that manner To network is to identify and cultivate a mutually-beneficial relationship - but the benefit can be different depending on the person and their needs. Think about networking as a cycle of social capital. Social capital is what you have to offer the people around you, and what they have to offer you. It includes a wide gamut of things from expertise and insight, to service, to opportunity, connection, influence and community.

If you think about networking this way, you are able to systematize what you can do, what you can deliver, and what you can gain. This form of structure provides clarity and direction, lending you greater confidence in how you approach people and nurture relationships. This change in mindset also lends you more power to positively impact others.

All too often we go to an event, listen to the talk, keep quiet, and run out as soon as the networking part begins because we are uncomfortable and eager to get home. My advice: "better to go to fewer events but invest fully once there".

This guide is designed to help build confidence and the right mindset to best present your smart, savvy, professional self. I encourage you to take the time to walk through this step-by-step guide to become a highly effective networker.

Now we get into the step-by-step instructions to add hustle to your networking activities and speak up your way to success.

You deserve your dreams.

1

IT ALL STARTS WITH YOU

I always believed you
could learn something
from nearly everybody
you meet, if you are
open to.

- HILLARY CLINTON

1. DISCOVER YOUR "WHY?"

Do you really know why you should go networking? To create a successful networking strategy, you need to be clear about why you want to network in the first place. If you don't know what you want to achieve, how can you use your network to achieve it? It is all fine and well to say, "I want to win new clients" or "I want to find a better job", but you'll need to be more specific about your end goals if you want your networking to be useful.

To help determine your networking goals, it's worth reflecting on your key reasons to network:

➢ **Driving recommendations:** The more people you know who know what you do, the more endorsements you will get online and offline (for example by word-of-mouth). Turn your connections into your [brand] ambassadors.

➢ **Encouraging mentors:** Through networking, you can often find successful people who are willing to share their experience, advice, and tips with you.

➢ **Raising your profile:** Surveys show that when you do a great job and you're visible, your chances of promotion are much greater.

➢ **Developing your current career:** Broaden your professional horizons. Networking keeps you current and in touch with your industry. Your career should never be stagnant.

➤ **Finding suppliers and market opportunities:** Networking is a great way to find the best suppliers and can help you identify new market opportunities you might not have thought of.

➤ **Building your knowledge in your industry:** Talking to new people can keep you up to date with your competitors' thinking, which you can use to your advantage.

➤ **Getting new ideas:** Meeting other people can encourage you to think outside of the box by exposing you to how people in the same industry or in other markets generate new ideas.

It's absolutely fine to network for all, some, or even just one of these reasons, so long as you are clear about your motivations and how networking will benefit you. Keep in mind that it is important to have a clear vision of your goals, otherwise you will be confused and will find it very difficult to spend time and energy on networking activities.

Now it's time to take these points and apply them to your personal case. Use the questions below as a guideline to create a list of reasons, and put them in order of importance.

• Are you networking to find new business opportunities, contacts, or introducers, or to retain and build existing relationships?

• Are you networking to find a sponsor or mentor?

- Is your networking activity for career development, such as finding another job within your company or another company?

- Are you networking to position yourself as an expert within your market or peer group?

- Are you building your network to set up a team of experts?

- Is your networking activity to increase your knowledge about your market, specific industry issues, or the factors that influence your customers' buying decisions?

- Are you networking in order to strengthen relationships with colleagues and employees and motivate your team?

- How much of your networking effort do you want to focus on finding new contacts and how much should be spent building relationships with existing contacts?

- How much of your networking effort should be spent developing internal relationships (colleagues and employees) and how much should you give to external ones (clients and contacts)?

- How urgent is each of your networking goals?

- Any other considerations?

REASONS TO NETWORK

Fill in the following chart with your answers (p88)

REASONS TO NETWORK	PRIORITY RATING (1=LOW - 10=HIGH)
Find new clients	7
Learn about my market	6
Find introducers	8
Increase my profile	9
Other reasons	

When considering your reasons to network, it's important to establish how much of your networking time and effort you should devote to your different goals. Networking doesn't have to take up a lot of time if you strategically consider what you are doing.

2. IDENTIFY "WHAT" TO DO

A clear and concise networking strategy will allow you to make the decisions as to 'what' networking activities you will do. Once you have determined your goals and found a couple of events or activities that you would like to join, write them down as your **networking action plan**. If you implement your networking plan, you will achieve your **networking goals**. You'll also be able to identify if your strategy is working, and figure out how to adapt it (ref. I.3 Make Time for Networking).

To set up your networking plan, you need to breakdown your networking priorities into activities and goals. Some of your networking relationships may be specific stepping-stones towards your medium and long-term goals. Estimate the number of contacts you will need to achieve your networking goals.

NETWORKING GOALS

Fill in the following chart with your answers (p89)

REASONS TO NETWORK	CONTACTS/ACTIVITIES	GOALS
Increase my profile	Join 2 key membership organizations to introduce myself/my business to 10 new people (5 in each organization) Connect with 5 influencers on LinkedIn	2 organizations 10 new people (5 in each organization) 5 influencers on LinkedIn
Find introducers	Already know 3 introducers; ask them for referrals Need to increase introducers to 6	3 new introducers
Find new clients clients	Contact 15 main clients and ask them for referrals and introductions Already know 10 potential clients; develop better relationships	15 clients 10 potential clients
Learn about my market	Speak to 3 existing suppliers Find 3 potential suppliers about new products Research 4 competitors and find out about pricing, marketing strategies, customer base	3 suppliers 3 potential suppliers 4 competitors

Approximately 53 contacts needed to achieve my goals

Setting clear goals, then identifying the objectives needed to achieve those goals, will provide you with much clearer insight to determine what you actually need to know or learn from someone. Having these goals established before you attend the event will also ensure that you are using your time productively. It will help you decide whether the event is a profitable one for you and will help you determine whether to attend it regularly or not.

3. MAKE TIME FOR NETWORKING

➤ **One hour a week:** This is the smallest amount of time you need to spend - on average - consuming social networks: scanning business news almost every morning.

➤ **Four hours a week:** In this amount of time, you can contribute actively to your business community with social networking activities like sharing relevant business articles every day, organizing a monthly networking event or arranging for a speaker to come to your workplace, and initiating a weekly one on one networking lunch.

➤ **One day a week:** By making such a commitment to networking, you set out to significantly raise your profile in your business community to that of a thought leader by: writing one opinion piece a month and getting it published on prominent industry blogs, giving talks at industry events, and making connections within your network that have the potential to turn into win-win business partnerships.

In order to have a clear picture of what your networking activities should look like, detail your actions as much as possible in your Networking Action Plan.

NETWORKING ACTION PLAN

Fill in the following chart with your answers (p90)

Specific plans and commitments this month:

Block off time in your calendar each week to network	Make a 2x2 list
For example, every Wednesday at lunch or every Monday after work.	Make a plan to meet with two people that you already know and two people that you don't know. Call or email these people to see if they would be interested in meeting with you over the next few weeks.

Research professional organizations and sign up for one this month	Try a new social activity
Do some research online to find the best professional organization in your area for your industry. Go to a meeting this month and find someone at the meeting that you enjoy talking to.	Join a sports team after work, take up a new hobby, or attend a new church where you get to meet other people. Whatever you do, make new connections!
Plan ahead for your 4 x 4 for next month	**Check back in with the person who is holding you accountable**
If you plan out NOW who you are going to meet with next month, you will easily meet with 8 people and enjoy it because you won't be stressed. So start emailing your growing network!	Review your goals, seek advice and be honest! Let your accountability partner know how you are doing with your networking plan and what you need help with.

Make/update your master list of all of your contacts	Follow up
Put reminders in your calendar every month to make sure you stay on top of birthdays and other important events. This way you will be ready to send out Christmas, birthday, thank you or job search update emails to your network to stay in touch.	Send an email to everyone that you have met so far and thank them. Be sure to thank all of the people who have opened up their networks and connected you with their friends and co-workers. Be generous and let them know how they helped you!

Write down what you learned this month
Re-evaluate your networking plan goals and decide if you want to go a different direction next month.

> What is working in my network?
> What is not working in my network?
> Where am I overinvested in my network?
> Where am I underinvested in my network?

IT ALL STARTS WITH YOU

Summary Action Steps

- Write down the main reasons you want to network and prioritize them.

- Identify your networking goals and set up clear steps to reach them.

- Set up time in your calendar for your networking activities.

<u>NOTES</u>

2

PREPARE YOURSELF FOR SUCCESS

> Networking is like exercise. You know you must, but do you? And you know if you do, you'll feel better.
>
> - CANDACE CORLETT

As a woman, have you found it hard to be seriously taken by men? Have you ever faced a situation when, while talking business to a male counterpart, he thought that you would be interested in dating? It is frustrating, isn't it? On the other hand, it can be also difficult to deal with other women because, like it or not, we can be tough on one another. When a problem arises and gets in the way of good networking, good networkers don't get overwhelmed; they look for solutions. Proper preparation and planning before networking events will help you to alleviate any fears you might have and overcome any bad experiences you may encounter. It is easy to do if you follow a few simple steps.

1. IMPROVE YOUR PUBLIC PROFILE

In today's ever competitive and challenging market place, it is necessary to tell the world who you are, what you do and what area of expertise you have. There is a variety of social media to showcase who you are and LinkedIn is (so far) the best online platform to increase your professional profile. The beauty of online visibility is that you decide what you want others to know about you - you control the narrative.

For LinkedIn, have an updated list of experiences and qualifications for people to get a real sense of how your career has progressed to date, and what they can expect from you. Twitter and Facebook are other great platforms to showcase your personality and exercise your point of view on issues you find interesting. Make sure your social media profiles are a strong reflection of your interests and the network you aspire to build. Instagram is the platform to showcase your work and express your creativity.

2. DO YOUR HOMEWORK BEFORE YOU GO

Regardless of the type or size of the event, you want to get the most from the time you spend networking. Part of having a plan is knowing not every event needs attending, and feeling secure when you turn down the occasional invitation.

Doing some simple preparation before you rush out the door will improve your results from the events you choose to attend. Think about how you can best achieve your objectives and what preparation may be necessary:

➤ Find out what the event is about and what the audience will be like.

➤ Make a list of current clients, prospects and/or contacts who might be interested in attending, and send them a quick email a few days before to let them know you are going and to ask if you will see them there. If it's someone you haven't seen in a while, let her or him know that you are looking forward to catching up. Try to think of a connection you can make that could be of benefit to them. Remember: generosity is the key to success.

➤ Set up meetings. If there is a list of attendees who will be at the event, double check to see if someone you are interested in connecting with is registered. You might even want to call or email this person in advance to set up a meeting during the event. Check your database for contacts in the area where the event is located. You may find that you know people who live or work nearby who won't be at the event, and you can make an appointment to reconnect with them, too.

➢ Do a little research on each of the people you want to meet. A little knowledge goes a long way. If you know something about the people you approach, it's much easier to start a conversation and keep it going.

➢ Focus on the quality, not quantity. You will get better results by making a few good connections than by handing out dozens of business cards indiscriminately.

➢ Prepare questions. Even if you are going to a breakfast, luncheon or dinner event, take a few minutes to formulate a couple of relevant questions you can ask.

➢ Set a goal for the event. How many people do you want to meet? Who do you want to meet? How many referrals or introductions do you want to make?

➢ Be prepared to answer the most popular networking question of all: "So, what do you do?"

3. LEARN TO TALK ABOUT YOURSELF

The ultimate key to networking success is authenticity. Some people make the mistake of claiming skills and works that they do not own to make a good impression. Do not fabricate stories or an image because you think it's what you need to earn someone's trust or respect. You don't need to pretend to be someone that you are not. What impress people is when you show a willingness to share your story. What earns their respect is when you are thoughtful in your actions.

If you are guarded, people don't have the opportunity to learn what really makes you, you. Bring your smartness and uniqueness to light. Being true to people will allow you to maximize the true essence of networking, which is human connection.

A great tool to develop is an elevator pitch. It is a brief message that covers the who, what, where, when, and why. Consider an elevator pitch to be a bite-size commercial that provides people as much information as they need at the time to make an informed decision about who you are, what you are looking for and how you can benefit a company or organization. An elevator pitch is handy because you can whip it out when you least expect a professional encounter, like having a run-in at a cocktail party, the grocery store or the gym. To help you craft the perfect elevator pitch, consider the following five elements:

Fill in the following chart with your answers (p93)

YOU	Who are you? What are you passionate about? What do you want to achieve in life? What can you deliver? Be creative!
YOUR CONFIDENCE	What makes you the best at what you do? If you say that your skill set is in sales, no one will doubt you. However, if you expand on this by explaining that you have "a knack for persuasive selling", you are more likely to catch people's attention. Your concise and clear understanding of your abilities will not only lead others to believe in your competencies but also help potential clients or employers identify how you might meet their needs.
YOUR GOAL	What do you want? Really consider what result you want from the interaction: is it to find new prospects? Is it to learn new information in your industry? Is it to pick someone's brain about best practices in your field? Don't be afraid to make 'the ask'; your elevator pitch positions you as a solution.
YOUR MOTIVATION	What's your "why"? While it isn't necessarily unspoken during your elevator pitch, your "Why" is the most important aspect of your pitch as it allows you to create a connection and find common ground with people. Finding your 'why' will help keep you inspired and motivated to take action.

Boom! And there you have it, a concise and powerful message that gives you the power to articulate who you are, what you do and why you do it. Be prepared to adapt your pitch accordingly based on the person you are speaking with and the context in which that conversation is taking place.

So now that you know what to put in your elevator pitch, let's discuss what **NOT** to do.

➤ **Speak too fast:** Ok, you may only have 30 to 60 seconds to make your pitch, but try to avoid to put too much information into that one minute.

➤ **Use highly technical terms:** You want your pitch to be easily understood by any audience; that means keeping it simple. The last thing you want is for whomever is listening to feel dumb.

➤ **Not being focused:** This is not a casual conversation or small talk. Keep your pitch clear and focused.

➤ **Not practicing your pitch:** First, write down your pitch. Read it over and over again. Have your friends and family read it. Does it make sense to you? Then practice it. Practice it again. Keep practicing it until it becomes so easy for you to pitch that it feels completely natural.

➤ **Not saying anything:** It does absolutely nothing for you to have a killer elevator pitch if you never use it.

Now it's your turn to craft your own elevator pitch. Remember, keep it short and keep it simple.

4. PRACTICE POSITIVE PRESENTATION

By now you know that networking is about forming meaningful connections. Because you are trying to grow your network, chances are that you are planning to attend more than a few conferences and networking events to speed up the process. But just showing up and passing out business cards isn't the way to build relationships. You need to make sure you have the right body language and conversational tools to set the stage for a positive interaction.

When it's time to mingle, reminder:

➤ **Your smile:** The power of your smile is unlimited. It conveys openness and confidence and makes you seem approachable.

➤ **Your handshake:** Firm handshakes communicate confidence and power. Weak and flimsy handshakes communicate just that weakness and being overly soft (not suitable for a fast-paced, highly demanding environment).

➤ **Breath mints:** The quickest way to turn someone off is to kill them with your breath. You may have the best elevator pitch, but if the person just wants to get away from your foul breath, they are not listening to what you have to say.

➤ **A plan:** This takes you back to your networking strategy and your activity plan. Having a plan helps you stay focused on the objective: people you want to meet, the number of follow-ups you hope to receive, etc.

➤ **An icebreaker:** Making the first move can be daunting, but it doesn't have to be. Remember that people are here to meet others, just like you. To build rapport quickly, it is always easiest to start with non-business topics. You can start any conversation with some "small talk" about the event, the weather, if the food is good. Please don't spend more than 1 or 2 minutes talking about the weather. It's wasteful. Once you have broken the ice, ask insightful questions. Often, the person you're approaching will appreciate that you've chosen to speak to them, and as long as you're courteous and being yourself, you'll create a positive impression. Make an honest effort to learn about who they are and what has led them to the same event.

➤ **Your elevator pitch:** This is a great time to put your elevator pitch to good use!

➤ **Your business cards:** Don't pass your business cards around; it may give people the impression that you are only interested in pushing your business information. Hold onto your business cards and give it only if you feel like you want to develop the relationship with the person you are talking to.

➤ **A pen and notepad:** Take notes. Immediately following the event, write a brief note with the helpful information you gathered. These details will quickly fade in the days following an event, so taking physical notes is a good way to remember who is who, what they do and how you are planning to take the connection to the next level.

5. DRESS APPRORIATELY

Before you walk into any networking events, make sure you are dressed appropriately. When you go to a networking event, you have an opportunity to present yourself in the way you want to be perceived by others. Whether it is a one-on-one meeting with your future mentor or a social time after a conference, keep in mind that you have less than 5 seconds to give a first good impression. Make no mistake about it: you are being evaluated.

It is possible to strike a balance between presenting yourself professionally and showcasing your personality. What you wear at a networking event can be a "conversation starter". For example, at a more formal gathering, feel free to glam up with a necklace or broach to add some character to your outfit.

On the less glamourous side, you may encounter situations where you receive sexist comments. To stop unwelcome advances, dress professionally, have a firm handshake and under no circumstances flirt. It will cause more damage than it could help. Dress in the way you wish to be addressed.

PREPARE YOURSELF FOR SUCCESS

Summary Action Steps

- Increase your profile with a curated online presence.

- Get rid of ambiguity (and awkwardness) with some prep before your next event.

- Learn to talk about yourself in a positive and remarkable way. Stay true to yourself and be honest.

- Prepare icebreakers and open-ended questions.

- Dress the way you want to be addressed.

NOTES

3

WORK THE ROOM

Don't be intimidated by
what you don't know. That
can be your greatest
strength and ensure that
you do things differently
from everyone else.

- SARA BLAKELY

Networking events are often full of people you don't know, and striking up random conversations is not easy for most of us. Just focus on the positive. You are here to meet new people, discover new things and have fun. If you have taken your preparation seriously, once you walk into the room, this is the time where you get to have some fun and demonstrate your preparedness. Recognize the work you've put in, celebrate the clarity you've gained and entertain the experience with a sense of self-assurance and humility.

➢ **Enter with confidence:** Even if no one's watching you, expressing an air of confidence will make you feel more confident. Sometimes, confidence is a "fake it 'til you make it" kind of game. So, dress your best, strike a power pose, and walk into that room with the mindset that you are going to rock this party.

➢ **Don't stick to people you know:** If you are attending the event with people you already know well, such as colleagues and friends, don't fall into the trap of sticking together for the whole event. Talking to people who you already know will lessen your chances of meeting new ones. To extricate yourself, deliberately sit next to someone you don't know during a talk or a meal that takes place during the event.

➢ **Don't waste time** in groups where you have nothing to gain: Simply excuse yourself and leave.

➢ **Watch your body language:** It is difficult to start a conversation with someone looking at the floor with crossed arms. Keeping an open posture, head up, arms and legs uncrossed to convey openness to being approached. Body language plays a significant role in the way in which you communicate.

➢ **Give a good handshake:** It shows that you are friendly, interested (and interesting!), and projects more of that confidence we talked about earlier. Always keep your drink in your left hand to keep your right hand free and dry.

➢ **Give your full attention:** It's tempting to continue scanning the room while you talk with someone, but this is a great way to make that person feel uncomfortable or simply walk away. When you are with someone, give them your full attention, just as you would expect them to do with you.

➢ **Remember people's names:** Remembering names is a sign of respect. However, if you are like me and have trouble remembering the names of people you first meet, this may be challenging. We have all been there; you are having a nice conversation with someone you just met and suddenly you realize you have forgotten their name. Don't feel too embarrassed. Actually, there are a few things you can do to avoid it. When they introduce themselves, say their name back to them: "Nice to meet you, Jane". If their name is unusual, ask them to pronounce it, or spell it for you, even if you got it right the first time; this will help you remember it later on. Use their name a few times when addressing them in conversation to help keep it top of mind.

➢ **Move on graciously:** At some point you must move on to meet other people. If you've spotted someone, ask if the person you are talking to would like to be introduced.

If your cup is empty, offer to fetch a refill. With these two examples, you give the other person the option of staying or going. Most of the time they will want to move on, so they will decline your offer. If they do accept, you'll inevitably introduce them someone else. Whichever, there is no embarrassment. In a situation where you feel stuck, you can say ,"Come on Jane (or Mary, or Henry…), let's go and meet some others". Simply take them with you and include them.

➢ **Manage rejection:** Getting ignored or treated rudely can be the worst part of networking. I remember a networking event when a man approached me. He was deep in discussion with his colleagues (a group of men) and reached out to include me, very nicely asking if I would like to join their group. While I was greeting the others, the man asked if he could offer me a drink. Of course! I would like a juice, please. He wondered if I wouldn't prefer alcohol, but I declined. An orange juice will be fine, thank you. I could read on his face that he was not happy with my choice of beverage. I thought it would be okay and that I could still talk to the other members of the group. But it didn't go that way. Instead, after I turned down a drink of alcohol, the entire group turned their back on me. I was not welcome anymore. I remember feeling sick, I was so upset. I didn't say a word and left the event. I didn't want to talk to anybody else. You may think as many rude thoughts as you like, but when networking you must keep your composure and poise. To overcome this kind of situation, take a deep breath and think about who you are. You're a likeable person, you have been polite and courteous in your approach, you're well qualified in what you do, and there are a lot of people who would love to connect with you. Stay focused on your objective.

> **Read the body language:** When it is obvious that the person with whom you're talking isn't interested and looks over your shoulder or glance around the room, do them and yourself a favour, and move on.

Going to a networking event you know that you will be speaking with new people, so bring your best self! People will enjoy speaking with you and be curious to learn more about you if you are friendly and ready to mingle. A good way to immerse yourself in a positive atmosphere is to do something that makes you happy before heading into the event, whether that is listening to your favourite music, or getting a delicious coffee, do something that will make you in your best mood.

WORK THE ROOM

Summary Action Steps

- You are here to meet new people, discover new things and have fun.

- You can't escape rejection. But you can let it go. Fear of rejection is not a helpful emotion in business as it's not personal.

- Keep your networking goals in mind.

- Analyse people's body language and feedback.

NOTES

4

BUILD HUMAN CONNECTIONS

> Many receive advice, only the wise profit from it.
>
> - HARPER LEE

BE ENGAGED

Networking is all about building relationships based on appreciation, trust and giving. Having useful connections can lead to rare opportunities. Remember your role is to add value to your circles and contribute to your community.

As you network, focus on asking people about themselves and their work. View networking as a time to learn more about others and share your story. Here the objective is to foster a real connection. Some helpful tips to engage with purpose include:

➢ **Ask insightful questions:** Don't limit yourself with one question "What do you do?". There is a lot more to a person than their title, industry, or company name. Instead, ask questions about the person. That could be, "what are you working on that's exciting right now?". Bare in mind that the only way to find out about people's business and their challenges is to ask questions that allow them to light up a bit and connect as humans, not as talking business cards. At this point, you cannot create need, you can only spot potential opportunities.

➢ **Pay attention:** This may come naturally for some people, and can be difficult for others. In our smartphone era, paying attention is a demanded "skill" many people lack. By maintaining eye contact, listening attentively and responding with relevant questions, you are separating yourself from the crowd and are on your way to fostering a genuine relationship.

➤ **Be kind:** You never know what will come out of your meetings. When connecting, be direct but never pushy or arrogant.

➤ **Ask how to get in touch:** "What is the best way to get in touch later in the week?". Your new contact will let you know her/his preferred method, whether it is a phone call, an email or another way. When you know the answer to this question, it's much easier to follow up.

Make sure that from the moment you arrive to the time you leave, you are engaged with the right people and are having relevant conversations. Don't worry if you are the youngest person in the room or have the least amount of professional experience. If you bring a unique perspective and speak up, you are a valuable asset.

BUILD HUMAN CONNECTIONS

Summary Action Steps

- Networking is all about building mutually beneficial relationships.

- Ask people about themselves, their passion, their work.

- Find common ground to facilitate the conversation.

- Don't forget to ask how to get in touch.

NOTES

5

MOVE THE RELATIONSHIP FORWARD

It's fine to have friends, but quality relationships plus strategy should be your goal in business.

- JUDY ROBINETT

This is everything you have been working towards: you attended a networking event, you met some nice people, you found potentially interesting opportunities. Now it's time to build those connections.

Business cards have no value if you don't use them, so this chapter will help you maximize their use. A networking event is just the starting point of a new relationship; your follow-up is the key to developing it.

1. FOLLOW UP

> **Send a quick email:** Send a follow up email within 48 hours. Simply say that you enjoyed meeting them and try to reflect back on a point from the conversation. For example, "It was so nice to meet you at the Chamber of Commerce event last night! Best of luck with your daughter's basketball championship this weekend!" In order to move forward you might add, "we started to talk about the synergies we have in our prospecting and I'd love to continue that conversation. How does your schedule look next Thursday for a coffee or lunch?" It doesn't have to be long or formal, but you need to initiate the next step. When scheduling the first one-on-one meeting, be clear about your intentions beforehand so the other party can prepare accordingly.

> **Connect on LinkedIn:** The LinkedIn platform offers so many opportunities to keep your contacts front-of-mind for you (and you for them). Indeed, whether it is a pop-up in your email on their birthday, a notification when they have a work anniversary, or an announcement when they

get a new job, this social media took gives you numerous occasions for follow-up. So after you have met, ask to link up on LinkedIn.

2. KEEP IN TOUCH

It's time to go from being someone your contact met once at a conference to someone they look forward to hearing from. Do not lose sight of why you made an effort to connect with any given individual. Remember to be of help; don't just ask for it.

➢ **Be prepared:** Ask relevant questions and to answer any questions. Be alert from the moment you arrive; you may pick up some useful information just by observing. Once again, it shows that you're genuinely interested. It might be something you've just seen at the reception or in the office (family photos, certificates, trophies, plaques). If you're struggling for topics, go back to the networking event by saying something like, "it was a really good event the other day, don't you think?".

➢ **Don't sell, let them buy:** As you proceed through the meeting, ask yourself: is there a real problem that needs a solution? Are they unable to find the solution? Are they in a position where they are ready to take action? And so on. If you get positive signs on all of the above and you believe you can help, then you can go into your presentation and position yourself and/or your services as a solution. Put in plain words as briefly as possible what you can offer, what the process would look like, and what is likely to happen.

3. MAINTAIN YOUR SOCIAL CAPITAL

➤ **Become a resource:** Always look for opportunities to support someone, even if you don't receive an immediate return for your effort. Remember that networking is about giving first.

➤ **Create a "reconnect" file:** The more relationships you build, the more likely you will create new opportunities. After you have a follow-up meeting or phone conversation with a new contact, I suggest you create a "reconnect" plan using Excel or Google spreadsheets. It will help you to keep track of with whom you have been in touch and who is falling further away from your network. Generally, 3 months is the longest you want to wait before reaching out to someone again.

MY RECONNECT FILE

Name	Met At	Last Contacted	Contact Every...	City	Info to Remember	Next Steps	Contact Next
Jane Doe	New York Chamber of Commerce event	09/20/2017	month	NYC	is looking for a new job in accounting. introduced me the manager of company XYZ likes volley-ball	Ask for her resume and pass it on the accounting company Follow with the manager of company XYZ	
John Doe	Work Christmas dinner	07/11/2017	3 months	Toronto	has started a new business in accounting	Invite her/him to next event	

You might plan to connect once a month and include some information about how you met and what you have discussed in the notes. When that name pops up each month, reach out to catch up, maybe set up another meeting, or just send something that might be valuable such as an invite to another event, a great article, or an introduction to a useful connection.

During your initial meeting, did your new contact mention that her/his sibling was a job seeker? If so, maybe you can follow up and inquire about what they want to do, or ask for a resume to pass to a few possible connectors or companies who are hiring.

Your focus in reconnecting is to seek out opportunities through which you can help someone with a need. Take the lead and expect nothing in return and you will grow a positive reputation as someone who pays it forward. People will be attracted to you and will want to help you in return.

It isn't necessary to reach out to every contact every month, but it's a great way to keep your network active

4. USE THE POWER OF ONE CONNECTION TO OPEN MANY DOORS

Any contact with whom you interact knows hundreds of other people. This makes the power of your conversations exponential. Basically, when you are talking to someone, you are eventually speaking to their entire network. The same goes for them with you.

Once you have developed a new relationship with someone, you will want to be more intentional about how you help. If the person is looking for a job, a business lead, or some other tangible introduction, open up your list of contacts to them.

5. MEASURE IT

At the end of each month, before you decide to join another networking group or event, measure the results of your current efforts. This process is essential to see if your network is working, and to determine the best way to adjust it.

Make a list of all the groups you are in right now and ask yourself, "why am I in this group?". Write down your reasons. Do not join a group and just wait for things to happen only to walk away and say it didn't work. You get out of any group what you are willing to put in. Remember, networking is about giving.

There are four things you should be measuring:

TIME	
Building relationships that have a benefit to both sides takes time.	How much time have you invested in the group or with individuals?
GIVE	
It is important that you track the referrals you have given to others and the result of those connections.	How much business have you given to others?
RECEIVE	
This is key!	How many leads have you received?
RESULT	
This relates to RECEIVE. You may find out that the people you are giving good referrals to are only returning low level leads to you.	How much money have you made as a result of the leads you have received? How many of them were not very good?

Remember: if your network is not working, there is no growth happening and it is your responsibility to do something about it. If you didn't get the results you were expecting, take a look at what you may have communicated to them and then decide if you need to re-adjust or if you should move on. You always have the capacity to change your circumstances, but if you are not measuring your results, you will never know what needs to be done.

I suggest that you also re-evaluate your network by following the same process at the end of the year in order to get a better picture of your strategy and to set up better goals for the new year. I'm not talking about resolutions, but rather goals that you will commit to achieve.

6. SAY "THANK YOU"

Thanking your contacts for any help they may have given you is extremely important to continue the relationship. If you have received a referral that led to new business or got you a new job because of a connection, be sure to send a thank-you card or a gift to show your appreciation. Never take your network for granted.

MOVE THE RELATIONSHIP FORWARD

Summary Action Steps

- Follow up within 24h to 48h with the objective to solidify your relationship with your new contact.

- Be resourceful and offer your help.

- Keep your network active.

- Measure the effectiveness of your actions.

- Say "Thank You!"

<u>NOTES</u>

6

NETWORKING WITH THE OPPOSITE SEX

Without an open mind,
you can never be a
great success.

- MARTHA STEWART

1. WHY DO YOU NEED TO NETWORK WITH MEN?

The value of your professional network may depend on your gender. LeanIn.Org and McKinsey & Company found in a recent study that a woman's odds of advancement are 15% lower than her male counterpart.

One reason the study cites for this discrepancy is that women and men have very different networks. The study explains, "women and men agree that mentorship is vital to success and advancement, with two-thirds describing it as "very" or "extremely" important.

Now more than ever, men and women need to harness their networks to gain the business edge in order to thrive within our economy's competitive market.

Ladies, men make up 50% of the global workforce, so we cannot abandon consideration for how they work into our networks and affect how we navigate the workplace. What you may notice networking with men, especially those in your peer group or senior to you, is being on the defensive, a lot. The conversations tend to place you under spot light where you feel you are having to constantly validate your qualifications and prove your belonging or credibility. If you are working in a highly male-dominated industry you may find that more often than not, men do not trust your competency level off the bat. This is not entirely the fault of men, their upbringing is at fault too. What they see, they emulate. According to a study on career advancement by INSEAD, women have traditionally had to prove their competence, and cannot solely rely on their social capital. If men have seen their seniors engage in conversations with women that are constantly probing women to prove their self-worth, that expectation is understood as standard, and so the cycle continues.

First of all, keep in mind that the primary objective of a man's networking tends to be more business-oriented and less about friendship, while women tend to be less obvious when building their networks and rely more on relationships.

Secondly, whereas women are skilled at small talk but often don't move (comfortably) to the business talk, men want to get into business quickly. If and when you network with men, making a lot of small talk is not always necessary.

To be honest with you, I sometimes still find it hard to approach a group of people, and especially a group of men, at an event. I think women should always approach a group of men as long as they are standing in an open format. Give eyes contact to each, smile and ask if you might join them, and you will be welcomed in. Don't worry that approaching a man or a group of men is going to be taken the wrong way, as long as you remain professional. Men often use sport as an instrument for building relationships, whereas women find it easier to discuss personal information. Given this, consider knowing the bare facts about sports that are the most popular. A little knowledge about football or basketball can impress others and ease the discussion. If you still feel uncomfortable, approaching a mixed-gender group is always a safe option, as there is a mix of conversation styles.

To feel empowered in such situations, it is important to demonstrate ownership of the conversation and present yourself with strength and stride.

1. Make sure you're not always being the one who's being asked questions

2. Take men who support you to networking events that may be gender imbalanced

3. Highlight your wins

When spoken to inappropriately (little jokes, snide remarks, sexist comments), speak up immediately and let him know that what he said was not appreciated. You don't have to shout it. You can be professional while letting him know you do not expect such behavior at a professional event.

If you still feel overwhelmed, a good tip that I have learned is to leverage the restroom! *Yes, you can use the restrooms strategically*, even if you don't need to touch up your make-up. We - women - often chat in front of the mirror, so here you are. If you're struggling to make a connection, try striking up a conversation with another woman in the restroom. Take those 30 seconds to identify who she is, what she's looking for, and suggest you step outside to continue to the conversation. If we are going to be more successful, we have to approach each other with open minds and have a positive outlook, thinking something good will result from the hard work and focus we put into networking!

2. "WOMEN-ONLY" NETWORKING EVENTS ARE NOT THE SOLUTION

Here's an interesting yet contradicting question: do women-only networking events benefit women?

In a world when women have been disadvantaged for almost anything, and considering the barriers that professional and businesswomen face, it's no surprise to see women-only networks flourishing. But are they presenting an edge to help women network smarter? Are they proving to help women move up the corporate ladder?

Despite our efforts, networking continues to pose serious challenges for women. It's not that we aren't doing it. Women are attending more networking events all the time, and the number of women-only networking events grows every month. In a big city like Toronto, you can find dozens of networking events taking place each month. Research suggests women-only networking events are not as valuable for the following reasons:

> ➤ **Too much conversation, not enough action**

Many devote too much time complaining about the problems we face and far too little time on providing real, practical solutions to those problems. I firmly believe in the power of authentic conversation and sharing, but focusing solely on the chatting part soon becomes a waste of time.

> ➤ **A lot of sharing versus a specific ask**

One of the reasons women's networking doesn't often get us the results we want is that we're not clear and specific about the type of help we need. This is why having a networking strategy is essential. When you have identified the outcomes of your networking activity, you know why you are networking for, who you need to talk to and what you want to ask for.

➤ Providing emotional support when practical support is needed.

We're in networking groups to network. If you haven't left a meeting with a plan to make and receive at least one introduction or follow-up meeting for one of your fellow attendees, you're not using your time and energy strategically.

➤ A network not as powerful as it could be.

It's not strategic to cut your audience in half by restricting it just to one gender and this choice can cause a major career disadvantage. The reality is that there are more men in executive level and frankly there are just more men in the business world. As a result, when women seek to build strategic relationships, most of the time they will need to connect with men.

I am not dismissive of the idea that we still need women-only networks. They provide support and represent an invaluable forum to share knowledge and experience in a safe environment. They can also open up a whole range of contacts, from both within and outside your industry - especially in male dominated industry - which you may otherwise struggle to access. While women-only networks can provide value, you definitely need to go out of your comfort zone if you want to make some serious business moves. Otherwise, you're ripping off your chances of success.

Let's face it, when it comes to evaluating the effectiveness of women's networking groups, we don't set the bar high enough. And because collectively, we are just beginning to learn how to strategically develop alliances for mutual success, many of the networking events designed only for women lack the appropriate structure and systems-thinking needed to help women forge powerful relationships.

.

NETWORKING WITH THE OPPOSITE SEX

Summary Action Steps

- Approach people with an open mind and the desire to learn and accept different values.

- Be flexible.

- Do not cut your audience in half by restricting it just to one gender.

- When working in a male-dominated industry, bring a man colleague with you to ease the process.

NOTES

IN CLOSING

> Create the highest,
> grandest vision
> possible for your life,
> because you become
> what you believe.
>
> - OPRAH WINFREY

Without strategy, execution is aimless. Without execution, strategy is useless. I didn't write this book to motivate you. Motivation without action leads to self-delusion. This book is for the doers, the go-getters.

Listen, networking doesn't have to be scary. At first, as with any new activity, it may take a little while before you feel 100% comfortable. But as long as you follow the process outlined in this guide and approach networking with a positive mindset, you will improve your networking outcomes.

JUST DO IT

Networking is a lot like nutrition and fitness; we know what to do, the hard part is making it a top priority. And the only way to become convinced that networking is a priority is to start doing it and see the results for yourself.

Networking can help you generate new opportunities, deepened connections with existing contacts, and learn useful information about your markets, resulting in more relevant services and leading to more business.

Strategic networking can be difficult for emerging leaders because it absorbs a significant amount of the time and energy that managers usually devote to meeting their many operational demands. That's why it is crucial to be aware of your networking strategy and to build your networking plan.

MAKE IT A GAME!

Assign yourself a mission, and track your points. This week, I will send out five emails to people from my last job. At this event, I will speak to five people I don't know, or to anyone wearing a black accessory. This month, I will write down 10 networking activities such as posting on LinkedIn, having lunch with someone instead of alone, etc.

It's absolutely essential that you find some way to get hands-on experience networking as you search for employment, career growth, or new clients. Whether you volunteer for a church, non-profit or school, or find temporary or unpaid work, you'll want to get the proverbial "foot in the door" to help make the case that you know more about networking than you have ever read about in books.

You don't need a large amount of money for growth, you need a networking strategy. The fact is that it's one of the most cost-effective routes to business and career development. Done well, networking can lead to meaningful opportunities. You simply need to put an extra effort to see exponential results. Yes, you can do it!

In that sense, The Smart Woman Guide to Networking helps you optimize your time for greater effectiveness. Networking does not have to be a hurdle to your personal and professional growth.

Networking may be necessary but it doesn't have to be stressful. The success you seek is a reality that already exists within you. Your actions are the way you express that reality; it's time to bring it to your outer world.

ACKNOWLEDGMENTS

I would like to express my gratitude to all those who provided support, offered comments, and assisted me in the editing, proofreading of this book.

Above and all, I want to thank my friends and family who supported and encouraged me on my journey.

ABOUT THE AUTHOR

Darine BenAmara
Founder/CEO The Smart Woman
contact@thesmartwmn.com

When I was 25 year-old, I chose to dedicate my career to supporting other women and this is the best decision I have ever made. Since 2011, I have been working with women from all corners of the world. Inspired by their courage and resilience, I launched The Smart Woman, a platform focused on leveraging networking and leadership skills to support women's economic empowerment.

This book is a part of The Smart Woman brand, but it was quite a personal project. I truly enjoyed putting this guide together for you. Short but with some powerful goals behind it, I hope this guide gives you the confidence you need to make a pivot and present yourself with pride. I worked through the process myself over the years in my own and continuous self-development.

Please share your feedback and experiences so I can continue to address them and reflect your stories in the content I create. I encourage you to share this guidebook with other women who you know, deserve their dreams.

We may work together one day but today, I truly hope that I've helped to clear the clutter, get some pre-work done and prepare a proper foundation to plant your seeds for personal and professional success.

We'd really love it, if you share a picture of the book, you with the book or working with the book on your social media channels. Please use the hashtag **#imasmartwoman** on all posts and comments so we can find you. Let's create a community of support and inspiration. The more people that can get the message and be inspired from this book the better.

Thank you for honoring me with your valuable time! I look forward to reading your success story.

With your success in mind...Darine

YOU MAY ALSO LIKE

EXPRESS YOURSELF WITH CONFIDENCE

Effective Communication Tips For Networking Success

Available on thesmartwmn.com

Talking to strangers won't be a source of stress anymore. When you download Express Yourself With Confidence, your mindset and communication skills will transform! This step-by-step guide covers everything you need to know in order to ace your first impression, start conversations with anyone and end a discussion graciously. We also take a look at your body language. Express Yourself With Confidence includes networking scripts done for you to knock down networking barriers and network your way to success.

You only get one chance to make a first good impression, so make it count!

BONUS

"There is No Force More Powerful Than a Woman Determined to Rise"

HOW TO SET UP POWERFUL AND ACHIEVABLE GOALS

Do you know the difference between a wish and a goal? Lots of us wish for many good things, but not too many of us see those good things happen in our lives because we've never turned our wishes into goals. We often set wrong goals and spend too much time achieving them, thus end up being unsuccessful and unhappy. A lot of people work hard, but they don't seem to get anywhere worthwhile.

There are many things women should accomplish. A woman with a goal and the drive to achieve it is a force to be reckoned with.

FIGURE OUT YOUR GOALS

First consider what you want to achieve, and then commit to it. Set SMART goals that motivate you and write them down to make them feel tangible. Then plan the steps you must take to realize your goal, and cross off each one as you work through them. By setting clear goals, you can measure and take pride in the achievement of them, and you'll see forward progress in what might previously have seemed a long pointless grind. You will also raise your self-confidence.

SMART stands for:

- ➢ **S**pecific/significant
- ➢ **M**easurable/meaningful
- ➢ **A**ttainable/action-oriented
- ➢ **R**elevant/rewarding
- ➢ **T**ime-bound/trackable

State each goal as a positive statement; express your goals positively. It is better to tell yourself "Execute this technique well" than "Don't make stupid mistakes". The following broad guidelines will help you to set effective and achievable goals:

1. Be precise: Set precise goals, putting in dates, times and amounts so that you can measure achievement. You'll know exactly when you have achieved the goal, and can take complete satisfaction from having achieved it.

2. Set priorities: When you have several goals, give each a priority. This will help you to avoid feeling overwhelmed and help to direct your attention to the most important ones.

3. Write your goals down: This crystallizes them and gives them more force. Look at them pretty much every day it will help remind you to say yes to things that will bring me closer to them.

4. Keep operational goals small: Keep the low-level goals that you're working towards small and achievable. If a goal is too large, then it can seem that you are not making progress towards it. Keeping goals small will offer you more opportunities for reward.

5. Set performance goals, not outcome goals: Set goals over which you have as much control as possible. It can be quite frustrating and discouraging to fail to achieve a goal for reasons beyond your control.

6. Set realistic goals: Most important, set goals that you can achieve!

Goal setting is a powerful process for thinking about your ideal future, and for motivating yourself to turn your vision of this future into reality. It helps you choose where you want to go in life. By knowing precisely what you want to achieve, you know where you have to concentrate your efforts. You'll also quickly spot the distractions that can, so easily, lead you astray.

YOU CAN ABSOLUTELY DO IT!

Keep your eye on your goals and the landmarks along the way serving as milestones on the path to your end goal. That relentless vision for your goal is what will help you achieve it. Everything you do, every step you take should be toward that goal. You are a powerhouse, don't let the haters or roadblocks get in your way. You are a strong, confident, independent and smart woman with a goal to achieve and you can absolutely do it!

With that kind of drive and determination, nothing can get in the way of you breaking every barrier and succeeding wildly and extraordinarily more than anyone ever imagined.

Rise up and start everyday with enthusiasm!

YOUR TOOLKIT

MY REASONS TO NETWORK

REASONS TO NETWORK	PRIORITY RATING (1=LOW - 10=HIGH)

MY NETWORKING GOALS

						REASONS TO NETWORK
						CONTACTS/ACTIVITIES
						GOALS

Specific plans and commitments this month:

Block off time in your calendar each week to network	**Make a 2x2 list**
Research professional organizations and sign up for one this month	**Try a new social activity**

Plan ahead for your 4 x 4 for next month	**Check back in with the person who is holding you accountable**
Make/update your master list of all of your contacts	**Follow up**

Write down what you learned this month	
Re-evaluate your networking plan goals and decide if you want to go a different direction next month.	
What is working in my network?	**What is not working in my network?**
Where am I overinvested in my network?	**Where am I underinvested in my network?**

LEARN TO TALK ABOUT YOURSELF

YOU	
YOUR CONFIDENCE	
YOUR GOAL	
YOUR MOTIVATION	

THE SMART *WOMAN*

Inspire. Educate. Empower

Connect with us

www.thesmartwmn.com

 @thesmartwmn

44240601R00057

Made in the USA
Middletown, DE
05 May 2019